Yep, That's My Mommy!

Yep, That's My Mommy!

Written by: Jean Mountain
Illustrated by: Ashley Finch

YEP THAT'S MY MOMMY

Copyright ©2021 Jean Mountain
All rights reserved. Neither this book nor any parts within it
may be sold or reproduced in any format without permission.

Written by Jean Mountain
Illustrated by Ashley Finch
Developmental Editing by Mary Taris
Editing by Megan Hoff
Graphic Layout by Jermaine Taris

Printed in the USA
First Printing 2021

Published by Strive Publishing
3801 27th Avenue North
Robbinsdale, MN 55422
www.strivepublishing.com

ISBN: 978-1-948529-14-3 (paperback)
ISBN: 978-1-948529-19-8 (hard cover)
Library of Congress Control Number: 2021940499

A WORLD WITH MORE BLACK AUTHORS

To inspire community collaboration in publishing stories to heal, teach, learn, and earn,
while building an ecosystem that embodies a rich Black culture and heritage.

www.strivepublishing.com

What educators are saying about Yep, That's My Mommy:

"This book is a personal account of how a mom explained being transgender to her child. This gives a short synopsis of what a young child might encounter with their peers and society about understanding gender identity. I would recommend this book to families with young children as a simple guide to engage in conversations about what it means to be transgender."

• Ali Dvorak, Kindergarten Educator, 27 years

"An essential piece of literature for every classroom. Families and people are different, and that's okay! This story opens windows and doors into the world for even the youngest readers."

• Anna Twardowski, Elementary Educator

"It is important for children to learn about gender identity. Children are now living in a world where they are more likely to encounter a transgender classmate or see someone on T.V., the awareness and media visibility has increased. It's never too early to teach children about diversity, children understand more than we realize. This book is an easy read and will benefit children and adults"

• Debra A. Ruff, Preschool Educator

This book is dedicated to David Davenport.

"Your daddy's here!"

"What?"

Miguel did not know what to say to his classmate.

"Mommy!"

"Miguel, your daddy's here!"

"That's my mommy!"

"I'm a transgender woman."

"I am Miguel's mommy, and my name is Ms. Mountain."

"Auntie Jean is here!"

"I can't believe how big the kids are getting!"

"I know girl, they grow up so fast."

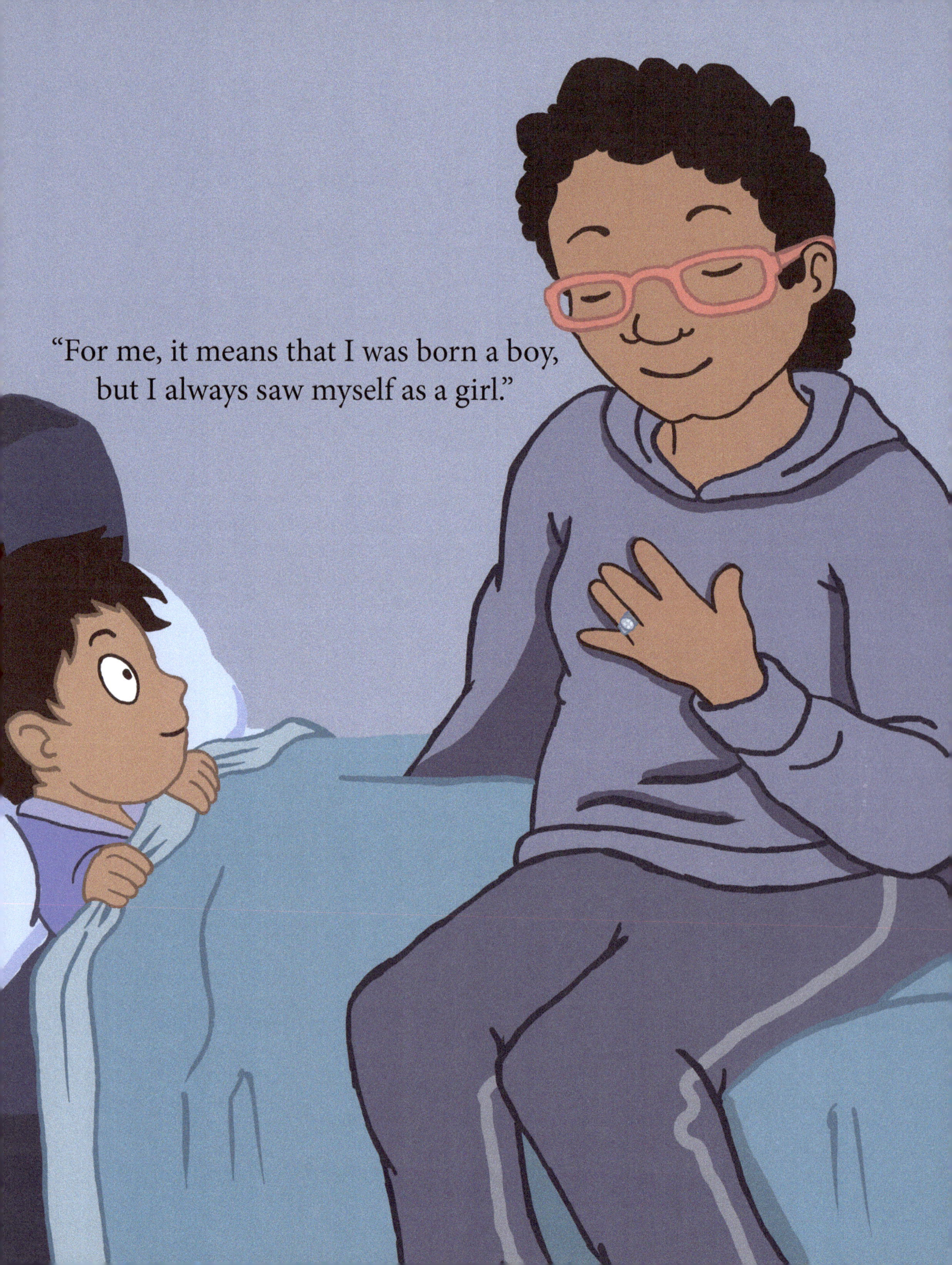

"Is it the same as Two Spirits?"

Extended Reading Activities

DISCUSSION STARTERS

Evaluate the author's purpose by completing this sentence: I think the author wrote this book to…

How do you think Miguel feels when other people ask about his mommy?

Who does Miguel remind you of?

Who does Miguel's mommy remind you of?

Why do you think the pronouns she, her, hers, he, him, his, they, them, theirs, are important?

How do you think we can make sure to use the right pronouns for people?

KEY VOCABULARY TO DISCUSS

Gender
Pronouns
Transgender
Two Spirit

LEARN MORE

National Center for Transgender Equality
www.transequality.org

About the Author

Jean Mountain, Author (She/Her/Hers)

Jean was born into a Native American family of fourteen children and raised on the northside of Minneapolis, Minnesota. She learned at an early age the struggle for a strong self-identity, from finding out she was Black to acknowledging her gender identity, to dropping out of high school. She believes it was her "street smarts" and big heart that enabled her to overcome those struggles and build a career as a home health aide.

Working in the home health care field for over 36 years has put Jean in the position to start a family and become a homeowner. She believes that God and honesty will get you what you need, not always what you want. She wants everyone to know there is hope and even without traditional education you can overcome with belief in yourself. "Not all that looks bad in life is bad. Be true to yourself and be true to your children."

As a transgender mother of four young children, Jean wants to teach families, educators, and the general public how to address her respectfully. As her children are getting older, she is seeing the need to show people how to treat them with respect and dignity. She wants to raise awareness of how others' reactions to her gender identity affects her children.

Jean wants everyone to understand that transgender mothers are mothers too, and that she loves her children the same way any other parents love their children. "In the end we all love our children the same."

About the Illustrator

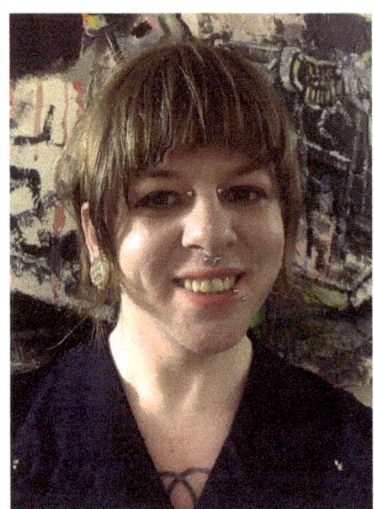

Ashley Finch, Illustrator (She/Her/Hers)

Ashley Finch is an artist and musician who loves science fiction, horror, and Americana. Since graduating from the College of Visual Arts, she has taught adult and youth art classes, and shown her illustrations in galleries and at academic conferences. She is currently working on multiple therapeutic and educational projects that aim to better the healthcare of trans-identified and gender diverse people. She lives in Saint Paul, Minnesota with her wife, her son, and a clowder of wonderful (yet at times troublesome) cats.

Aniin Boohzoo

I am Cynthia Mountain and from the Red Lake Reservation in Northern Minnesota. I graduated from University of Minnesota Twin Cities in 2019 in Indian Studies. In 2022, I graduated from the University of Minnesota Duluth in Tribal Administration and Governance. I am the first of my family to graduate from college, showing future generations, you are never too old to go back to school.

Here is the meaning of "*Two Spirit*", from the stories I have been told:

Two Spirit is a modern term used by Indigenous people of North America to describe Native people in their communities who fulfill a traditional third gender. The term *Two Spirit* was created in 1990 at the Indigenous lesbian and gay international gathering in Winnipeg. In history, *Two spirited* people were highly respected, which is why Native Americans use the term *Two Spirit* instead of Gay, lesbian or transgender.

Thank you for reading!

www.ingramcontent.com/pod-product-compliance
Lightning Source LLC
Chambersburg PA
CBHW041234240426
43673CB00010B/331